A Pocketful of PRESENCE

Carol LaRue

Copyright © 2024
All rights reserved.
ISBN: 978-0-9835070-1-7

It is my hope that you will keep this small book handy-in your purse, pocket, backpack, briefcase, bedside, or on your desk. I invite you to randomly turn to a page each week or day, reflect on how the message may apply to you, and integrate it into your life in your own way. Pass the peace along freely, by sharing it with a friend or loved one!

Wishing you peace, health, and resilience-
Carol

"Live in the moment. Know that moments are not in time. They are not in the world of the clock, the changing seasons, the process of growing old. Moments are soul time.

Wisdom is learning how to live in harmony with the world as it is in any given moment."

-Ram Dass

WONDER

Approach each moment with the innocence and wonder of a child. Be open to see and experience with fresh eyes, ears, and sensations the joy in the unexpected. Trust life and be available to all that it offers- moment by moment.

REFLECTION

What or whom can you approach today with fresh eyes and ears?

TRUTH

Allow yourself to exist in the world without becoming tarnished by it. Know your truth without pushing it on another, and accept what others find true for themselves. The only human you have full influence over changing is YOU.

REFLECTION

Is there someone or something you have difficulty accepting just as they are without judging or wanting to change them?

SPIRIT

Desires, thoughts, and intentions without *soul* resonance and conviction have no value. Invite the infusion of *spirit* into every cell of your body. Visualize and guide your body to *feel* what you wish to manifest.

REFLECTION

What would you like to manifest with your heart, mind, and soul?

Can you FEEL it, as if it were?

BEING

Take a moment to breathe and just be.

Being is the pause that calls forth your essence- the ever-evolving authentic vibration of your TRUE Self.

Be…with your being and listen intently.

REFLECTION

When was the last time you simply allowed yourself to BE, and allowed yourself to do nothing?

ENERGY

The vibration and radiance of your energy reflects:

How well you love.

How well you accept others.

How well you trust.

Your willingness to play.

Your ability to observe yourself.

Your balance of giving and receiving.

Your ability to sit quietly at peace with your SELF.

REFLECTION

If you could see your energy field, what color would it be? Does it feel open or closed? Does it attract or repel others?

PATIENCE

Patience is the practice of waiting while embracing uncertainty with a view of kindness and perspective within the moment.

When waiting, shift your attention to positive action- breath, conversation, meditation-and appreciate the time as a gift that is well spent.

REFLECTION

In what circumstances do you become impatient? How can you be more present in a 'waiting' situation?

BALANCE

A 'balanced' life is the result of staying centered in your soul's essence while being willing and able to adapt, shift, change, and grow in response to life circumstances with GRACE.

REFLECTION

Do you tend to resist planned or unexpected changes, or do you easily flow and adapt?

LOVE

When thoughts, words, and actions are formed from the seed of LOVE, they impact the universe with an energy of expansiveness- like 'open arms' inviting connection, acceptance, compassion, and understanding.

REFLECTION

Are there times when you find it difficult to love, accept, and understand? What examples can you think of? Can you have a 'change of heart'?

FREEDOM

Freedom is choosing to be right where you are while remaining open to the desires of your heart and mind.

Take time to 'hug' the fullness of who you are and where you are now.

REFLECTION

*Today be mindful of the freedom you possess to choose where the attention of your heart and mind goes.
What's your choice?*

AWE

Nature is full of 'AWE'.

Take time each day to pay attention to the 'AWE' of all that springs from the earth, the sky, the rhythms and cycles of the sun and moon, and the 'AWE' that you are part of it all.

Life. Death. Rebirth.

A never-ending cycle.

REFLECTION

Take some time today to notice the natural beauty in your world with a sense of wonder and awe. What do you most appreciate?

RESILIENCE

Reflect the *resilience* and the *balance* of Nature.

Breathe in the EARTH- Ground and Grow.

Breathe in WATER- Adapt and Flow.

Breathe in AIR- Lighten up and Laugh!

Breathe in FIRE- Ignite and Transform.

REFLECTION

Are you aware of how you reflect the elements of nature- earth, water, fire, and air? We are all of it!

MIND-BODY CONNECTION

Notice your thoughts.

Your thoughts create your world.

Your thoughts become
your feelings.

Your feelings manifest in your body.

Your body is home to your soul.

Create comfort for your soul.

REFLECTION

Notice how your body feels when recalling a stressful event. Notice how your body feels when recalling a pleasant experience. Which feels better?

NATURE

Embrace and find beauty in the long, dark, still, quiet nights of the winter months. Take time to prepare for the rebirth of light, the anticipation and joy of new beginnings, and the blessings of our natural world that spring forth.

REFLECTION

How can you better embrace the dark and cold of winter as an invitation to nourish yourself?

CHOICE

With every moment you have the power to choose what to focus on, what to accept, and what to release and let go of.

Choose to give attention to allowing your true self to be nourished and shine brightly.

REFLECTION

What choices are you making today that support and nourish your best self?

ACCEPT

No two trees or blades of grass are the same, yet we do not judge them, and we allow them to co-exist peacefully side by side in their unique beauty.

May we hold humanity with the same accepting heart.

REFLECTION

Of whom or what are you judgmental? Are you willing to seek greater understanding and become more accepting?

NATURE

Autumn is the time and rhythm when Mother Nature invites us to let go and seek comfort in what dies as it becomes rich, nurturing compost
for rebirth.

Let go of what is no longer life-giving for you, and surrender to renewed possibilities.

REFLECTION

Are you able to let go and trust a natural cycle of re-creation of what is most useful and fulfilling in your life?

LISTEN

Take time to go INWARD and allow your heart to speak to what matters and to what is most meaningful in your OUTWARD endeavors and energy expenditure.

Listen with love.

REFLECTION

How can you better take time to listen with your 'feeling' heart without letting your 'thinking' mind overrule?

TRUST

Control is an illusion. The best way to influence the outcome of any situation is to release your 'grip' and let go of expectations while opening up to possibilities. Trust, observe, allow, and adapt to the process- moment
by moment.

REFLECTION

Hold on tightly to a pen until your grip hurts. Now loosen your grip and flip, turn, and play with the pen while still holding it. In which scenario do you have the most control?

HEART

Your arms and hands are an extension of your heart's energy. Be mindful of extending and sharing tender touch, kindness, joy, compassion, love, and warm hugs-to others and your SELF!

REFLECTION

How often do you share your heart and extend loving touch- hold a hand or give a hug- to someone in your inner circle?

CURIOSITY

Be willing to step fully into the unknown with unwavering trust, vulnerability, and a courageous heart. Experience each moment with curiosity and an open mind.

REFLECTION

How often do you allow your curiosity to guide you into the unknown and trust that you will come away wiser?

BODY TALK

Discomfort and pain is our 'body talk'- a call to pay attention to and move blocked or repressed emotions. Avoid turning away from yourself and others.
Have compassion for yourself and seek compassionate companions for your healing walk.

REFLECTION

*Are you listening with compassion to
the messages your body is sending?
How can you show your body that you
are
paying attention?*

SELF-CARE

Self-care is a universal remedy for vitality, fulfillment, and resilience. Take time to reflect on how you will give your SELF the time and attention you need each day.

REFLECTION

In what ways do you tend to put the needs of others before your own? What time and attention do you need from yourself?

INNER PEACE

Your outer world reflects your inner world. Focus on settling into your breath and get comfortable with feeling stillness and peace. Feel more of what you want to create and see manifest in your world and the whole world.

REFLECTION

How often do you notice that you are holding your breath? How can you be more aware of using your breath to settle into the moment?

GROUNDING

Ground your feet on the earth.

Feel the fire of your desires and transformation in your belly.

Free your heart to be open, loving, and accepting.

Gently shine the light of your wisdom for others to see and know.

REFLECTION

How often do you catch yourself worrying about the future or the past? Your body is always in the now moment. How can you better connect to it?

NOW

When you process life as it is- in the NOW moment- rather than how you think it *should* be, you will experience true peace.

Be mindful of expectations of others without clear communication and understanding.

REFLECTION

Are you willing to trust that the NOW holds everything you need? Have you experienced disappointment through unmet expectations?

SELF-UNDERSTANDING

The simple act of noticing our thoughts and emotions without attachment gently guides us into the possibilities of the next moment and ignites our unlimited potential for growth and self-understanding.

REFLECTION

What have you learned about yourself through self-observation of your thoughts and emotions?

BEST SELF

Each moment holds the full potential of freedom of choice. Observe your choices. Mindfully choose the people, the information, activities, environment, and situations that bring out the best in you- so you can best love and serve the greater good
of the world.

REFLECTION

How are your choices of what you watch, what you eat, who you spend time with, and what you do, impacting your energy level?

KNOW

Set an intention for positive change in your life. Then, rather than *pushing* its creation into the busyness of the world, simply listen and follow the gentle *pull* of your silent, strong, inner 'knower'-guiding its manifestation in perfect timing.

REFLECTION

How often do you try to push and 'make' things happen rather than allow the manifestation of your intentions by stepping into openings of opportunity in perfect time?

CONNECTION

Notice and appreciate your spine, your legs, and your feet on the earth. Breathe deep into your belly while honoring your connection and time on this earth, your community and 'tribe' of family and friends- specifically those who support and bring out the
best in you.

REFLECTION

With whom or where do you feel like you most belong and trust that you will have the support you need?

GROWTH

Nature enjoys the freedom to grow and change in its own time. It does not hurry, yet everything is accomplished. When we slow down and are in rhythm with nature, it may actually
'hurt' to hurry.

Pause. Breathe. Slow down.

REFLECTION

Are there times when you feel like you are always hurrying or racing toward the 'next thing'? What would be the harm in moving a little more slowly?

FOCUS

Every thought influences how we feel- our emotions and our body. The moment we change our focus and perception, we change the chemistry of our being.

REFLECTION

How are you positively creating your experiences by what you focus on and how you interpret events? How is your body responding?

KINDNESS

Approach each day with kindness.

Choose love over anger.

Choose hope over frustration.

Choose unity over division.

You will never regret being kind.

REFLECTION

How does the level of your well-being reflect the kindness you give to yourself and others?

HAPPINESS

You are the master of your own happiness.

Stay physically active.

Nurture loving and supportive relationships.

Practice gratitude.

Spend time in nature.

Practice present moment awareness.

Be at 'home' within your SELF.

REFLECTION

What is your level of 'happy'? What do you need more, or less of, to increase your happiness? What's stopping you?

FLOW

Suffering occurs when we expect things to be permanent. *Everything* is temporary. Accept the flow of change in:

Thoughts

Feelings

Things

Time

Situations

Relationships

Life

REFLECTION

In what ways do you 'fight' to keep things as they are, rather than 'flow' with inevitable change?

GROWTH

When you quit growing, you die.

Living is growing.

Growing is changing.

Changing is learning.

Learning is experiencing.

Experiencing expands curiosity.

Curiosity feeds a fulfilling life and being in the NOW.

REFLECTION

How deeply are you committed to growing, learning, and living fully? How are you putting your commitment into action?

COMMUNITY

We *all* affect and influence our world. The vibration of our energy manifests in the universe by what we think, say, and do every moment. Every
moment matters because we are all *deeply interconnected*.

REFLECTION

In what ways are you aware of how your 'mood' and energy impacts those around you? How are you impacted by others in your environment?

SELF-CARE

Take time to be conscious of what you need to fill your own cup, so that you can best serve others. Self-care is
not selfish.

Nurture yourself through breath, movement, nutritious food, rest, and sleep. This is your only body for this journey on earth.

REFLECTION

How do you know when you are 'running on empty', and need to unplug from busyness and nourish yourself? What keeps you from doing it?

INTENTIONS

Your desires for your future are most effectively manifested by being in the present moment.

You may intend for the future, but your attention is in the present - focusing on the choices and 'right actions' now that contribute to your intention for
the future.

REFLECTION

Do you allow yourself to savor in the process -moment by moment- of manifesting your intentions or reaching your goals, or are you only focused on the 'finish line'?

GRATITUDE

Gratitude grows. It's like planting seeds- giving us more to be grateful for each moment and each day. Bring your heart and your brain into loving coherence by expressing appreciation, gratitude, and kindness.

REFLECTION

For what are you grateful? For what or whom are you appreciative? How do you show it or express it daily?

TRUE SELF

Tension, dis-ease, discomfort, and dissatisfaction can arise from trying to be what you or others believe you *should* be.

Take time each day to relax into *who you truly are-* reflecting on what brings meaning, ease, satisfaction, and fulfillment to your life.

REFLECTION

What activities or commitments seem 'hard' and create tension or feelings of dread? What is the 'why?' of your choice to engage in those?

POSSIBILITY MINDSET

When your thoughts, words, and actions are positive, loving, full of possibilities, and in alignment with what is true for you, you will create healing vibrations for yourself and the world around you.

REFLECTION

*Have you noticed times when you changed your mindset, (positively or negatively) and the world around you reflected
that change?*

SELF-EMPOWERMENT

Treat yourself kindly.
Put yourself first.
Forgive yourself.
Find and voice your truth.
Learn something new.
Do something that brings you joy.
Believe in yourself.
Dive into what really matters.

REFLECTION

*In what ways do you treat and advise
yourself as you would
your best friend?*

PERSONAL IMPACT

Our level of personal and professional connection, effectiveness, and impact is a direct result of our level of PRESENCE during everyday activities. Embodiment through our breath, and awareness of our sensations brings laser focus and connection to the NOW.

REFLECTION

What shifts in your effectiveness, connection, and efficiency do you notice when you stay present moment focused?

TRANSFORM

Personal awareness and mindfulness lead to positive transformation and change. As with the butterfly, one cannot 'push' the 'timing' of metamorphosis- for it is a natural and organic result of one's attention, shift in consciousness and chosen actions.

REFLECTION

Reflect on times when you have consciously created positive change with ease.

CALM

Connecting with the senses and sensations of the body can bring present moment awareness and calm to your being. Hum. Sing. Shake. Hug. Taste. Dance. Touch. Listen to nature. Laugh. Look closely. Breathe deeply and smell the moment.

REFLECTION

*Take a moment to appreciate your miraculous body. What sense or sensation do you most value and most readily
brings you calm?*

CONNECTIONS

The heart's remembering of those who have touched and influenced our lives brings forth an appreciation of who we are-a colorful tapestry of relationships, experiences, lessons, challenges, discord, deep love, and satisfaction. Give loving gratitude to all of it.

REFLECTION

Who are the people who have influenced your life in the past year? The past 5-10 years or more? Take time to feel the memories of their influences.

NATURE

How can you live more like Nature herself?

Your changing, adapting, transforming, and evolving and growing with grace reflects her wisdom.

Nature knows how to return to peace and balance following extremes.

Do you?

REFLECTION

*Do you recognize and appreciate the times when you have 'bounced back' from storms and disruptions in your life? How do you cope with events of stress
and chaos?*

SELF-LOVE

A loving heart naturally produces kind thoughts, kind words, and kind actions. Loving and respecting yourself and others is contagious. Breathe in love. Breathe out kindness.

Self-love is not selfish.

REFLECTION

How often do you take time to 'fill your own cup' with acts of self-love and self-care? Is it often enough?

APPRECIATION

A daily practice of gratitude immediately brings your heart and brain into 'positive coherence'. The practice of writing down what you are grateful for will attract more of 'what's working' in your life while creating more abundant manifestation.

REFLECTION

For what or whom are you most grateful for at this moment? Take a moment to feel the love and appreciation.

NOTICE

Be aware when you are running on 'auto-pilot'- moving from one thing to another without conscious awareness.

Pause.

Belly Breathe.

Reflect.

Reset.

Relax into Balance.

Return to Yourself.

REFLECTION

What can you notice differently today along a familiar road or during a daily routine or activity?

GRATITUDE

Every expression of gratitude will scatter seeds from which more to be grateful for will grow and flourish.

Plant your seeds of gratitude every day and enjoy the abundance that will grace your life.

REFLECTION

How do you express thoughts, words, and actions of gratitude?

SILENCE

Take moments to
Enjoy silence.
Enjoy observing without interacting.
Enjoy listening without speaking.
Enjoy the pleasure of a touch.
Enjoy savoring flavors.
Enjoy a pleasant aroma.
Enjoy feeling the rhythm of your breath and heartbeat.

REFLECTION

In what ways do you take time to notice and enjoy the beauty and pleasurable moments in silence?

FEELING

Emotions are neither 'good' nor 'bad'. Emotions provide information through our bodily sensations and responses. Emotions are simply ENERGY asking to be moved and expressed.

E-Motion…. energy in motion.

Move. Talk. Write. Release.

REFLECTION

What emotions do you find most difficult to express? Where do you feel those emotions in your body? How can you better 'move' those emotions?

WITNESS

Through the simple act of 'noticing', you can create positive change.

Notice what you are ruminating about.

Notice when you are racing around.

Notice when you are eating quickly.

Notice the depth and rhythm of your breath.

Notice the NOW.

REFLECTION

*What have you witnessed about your habits or behaviors lately that you would like to shift or change? What's the
first step?*

SACRED BODY

Honor and be kind to your body. It is a sacred entity, and the only vehicle for your soul's discovery and journey during your time on the earth.

Feed it well.

Move it well.

Rest it well.

Bring it pleasure.

Breathe energy into it.

REFLECTION

What are the ways that you hold your body in reverence and consciously give it positive attention and care?

BEING

If you feel stressed every day, you need to manage your stress every day.

When 'not doing' and taking a pause in incessant activity feels unfamiliar and impossible, it is a signal that you need it most.

Stop. Breathe. Rest.

Let go. Seek support.

BE.

REFLECTION

Does 'not doing' feel uncomfortable to you? Why? What positive habit or ritual do you have, or can you create to de-stress a bit every day?

CONSCIOUS CHOICE

Every choice you have made throughout your life has culminated in this moment - here and now.

Press 'pause' on your impulsiveness and open space for conscious, life expanding choices.

REFLECTION

What choices have been particularly pivotal in your present life and circumstances? How can you more consciously choose your future path?

CREATIVITY

The now moment perpetually re-creates itself. Your presence in the now creates never ending time and space for inspiration, creativity, joy, and meaningful connection with your
SELF and with others.

REFLECTION

How does worry or regret (focus on the past or future) interfere with your enjoyment and creativity?

MOVEMENT

How you move your body reflects how you move through life. Be aware of your movements and how you move.

Strong? Flexible? Joyous? Competitive? Hurried? Flowing? Rigid? Open? Slow? Quick? Light? Heavy? Graceful?

REFLECTION

How does your body feel when you move or engage in exercise or play? How can you infuse more lightness, ease, and flow into your movement?

NURTURE

Everything you 'ingest' or allow into your energy field holds potential for being *toxic* or *nurturing* for your whole being. Pay attention to food, information, self-talk, sights, sounds, and the people you surround yourself with.

REFLECTION

How well does your diet of information, relationships, environment, food, and rest nurture the well being of your body, mind, and spirit?

AMAZEMENT

'AWE' moments can spontaneously grace the heart of the observer. Open your heart to be in awe of the beauty of the natural world. Be in awe of the life-giving force of your breath and heartbeat. Be in awe of a child's smile and giggle. Be in awe of the possibilities awaiting you.

REFLECTION

*How often do you take time to be in awe? What or who creates those moments
in you?*

BALANCE

Honor and balance the 'yin and yang' and 'opposites' in life. We need it all.

Balance activity with rest.

Balance speaking with listening.

Balance giving with receiving.

Balance sound with silence.

Take pause.

REFLECTION

Do you tend to give more than you allow yourself to receive? Do you tend to fill gaps or silence with talking? How can you better balance activity with rest?

COURAGE

A satisfying life is created through your willingness to seek experience and dive into it.

Do things out of love rather than fear.

Practice gratitude.

Create positive change.

Try new things.

Be excited.

Challenge yourself.

Be fiercely brave.

REFLECTION

What is the most courageous thing you have done? How did it change you or your outlook on life?

SENSE

Fine tune your senses into the moment.

See, smell, touch, taste, and listen to the small, yet significant details in your world. What is soothing? What is harsh? What is distracting? Allow more pleasure, beauty, and comfort to infuse your being.

REFLECTION

How can you refine where your attention is directed to bring more comfort and pleasure into your being?

POWER

Acknowledge, embrace, and express your 'Superpower'. What characteristic, gift, or talent do you possess, that when expressed or put into action, produces a feeling of *timelessness, joy, pleasure,* and *immense satisfaction?*

Why not express it more?

REFLECTION

What is your superpower? What opportunities do you have to express and share it? Is it enough?

PEACE

Put a smile on your heart and on your face.

Be the instrument of peace that you are seeking.

Sow seeds of loving, kind energy within and let it shine through and all around you.

REFLECTION

Is your smile a true reflection of your feelings of peace, joy, and delight? How do you feel when you consciously smile more?

EASE

What you resist, will persist.

If something feels difficult, hard, or overwhelming, take a moment to pause and notice any resistance you may be creating out of fear or dread.

Breathe deeply and take one slow, simple step forward with ease.

REFLECTION

Can you recall a circumstance or project that you resisted or procrastinated on, yet when you finally stepped into it, it wasn't so bad after all?

LESS is MORE

Clutter can limit space for renewal and expansion.

Lovingly release and let go of thoughts, beliefs, habits, actions, commitments, belongings, and relationships that no longer serve your best self, your freedom, and your happiness.

Create space to attract what is most meaningful.

REFLECTION

*What do you need to clear out in your life that may be keeping you from growing into your most meaningful
and
rewarding life?*

ATTENTION

Pay attention to your attention. Notice on what, where, or whom you focus your time, attention, and energy.

Lovingly choose to give your attention to that which you want to see expand and grow in your life. Where attention goes, energy flows.

REFLECTION

Are you aware of directing your attention and intentions on what you want to experience more of in your life?
What is that?

PRESENCE

When you observe that you are not present, you *become* present.

When you observe where your attention is, you detach from the habitual mind.

Everything we really need is right here, right now.

This moment is as perfect as it can be.

REFLECTION

How do you feel right now? Can you trust the perfection of each moment?

JUST BREATH!

This QR code will direct you to a short video with simple instructions on 'Belly Breathing'.

This form of breathing not only triggers a relaxation response, but also brings attention and energy into our body's center of gravity, which helps with grounding and presence.

Carol LaRue is a licensed occupational therapist, international speaker and trainer, integrative wellness coach, and author of the book, The Art of Self-Health, Creating Total Well-Being from the Inside Out. Her training and practice in the field of holistic health and wellness spans over 30 years and includes experience in providing various forms of mindfulness exercises and movement, stress management education and training, wellness coaching and training, and facilitating group retreats and workshops. She is founder of LifeCentrics LLC, and is committed to assisting organizations and individuals of all ages in building resilience through mindful living. You can visit her website at: www.artofselfhealth.com